EMERSON *and* FROST

Critics of their Times

EMERSON *and* FROST

Critics of their Times

BY

LAWRANCE R. THOMPSON

FOLCROFT LIBRARY EDITIONS / 1973

Library of Congress Cataloging in Publication Data

Thompson, Lawrance Roger, 1906–
    Emerson and Frost; critics of their times.

    1. Emerson, Ralph Waldo, 1803–1882. 2. Frost,
Robert, 1874–1963. I. Philobiblon Club, Philadelphia.
II. Title.
PS1638.T5 1973   810'.9   73–182
ISBN 0-8414-1381-9

EMERSON *and* FROST

Critics of their Times

BY

LAWRANCE THOMPSON

---
*   *   *
....

An essay read before a meeting of the Philobiblon Club at Philadelphia on 24 October 1940, and now privately printed for the Members of the Club.

....
*   *   *

Philadelphia

The Philobiblon Club

MCMXL

THERE has never been a time of crisis and confusion that seemed to afford leisure for sober reflection and thought. "The times that try men's souls" are too often the times that try men's muscle, brawn, and instinctive will to survive by hook or by crook. If story books tell us of days when armies were led to battle by a poet lustily singing the saga of ancient heroes, we are inclined to relegate such pretty nonsense to the dusty shelves of romance. Our concern is with realism and hard-headed practicality. Poets are better understood as dreamers who live in a world apart, where they may press the heart to a thorn and sing their wistful regrets for vanished days and unrequited love.

If these dreamers concern themselves with the relation of the individual to society, and with the consequent social and economic problems of modern times, as Emerson and Frost have done, then we tolerate them condescendingly as well meaning but sentimental idealists, easy optimists, too far removed from realities to know what the real problems are. If these idealists embody philosophic ideas in their prose and poetry, as Emerson and Frost have done, we criticize them for this method of escape from everyday confusion by losing themselves in the intricate labarynth of metaphysics. Who could examine the benign composure of Emerson's half-smiling face and then conclude that Emerson could be hard-headed in his reasoning? Who could look into the Olympian serenity of Frost's eyes and then decide that Frost could be practical in his thinking?

But while there is still a little time for sober reflection and thought, let us look at those faces again. After all, their Yankee heritage of practicality and their years of living close to the soil should have taught them something about the problems of earning a living; the problems of getting on with neighbors. Since they took the trouble to be plainspoken in their criticism of the American scene, and since they spoke out not only in poetry but also in prose, perhaps they deserve to be taken seriously as critics of their times.

Furthermore, they stand not only as products of American democracy but also as representatives of what we like to believe to be the American spirit. Perhaps to get better acquainted with Emerson and Frost is to have a better understanding of the basic roots from which this nation has grown, and of the persistently vital direction of that growth.

The similarity between these two poets—perhaps the most permanent poets who have yet appeared as products of our American democracy—is the more striking when we discover their independence from each other. Emerson, of course, died before Frost had finished grammar school. And Frost never stayed in school long enough to read much of Emerson's writings. He admits that he has never bothered at all with Emerson's prose essays because he believes that the essence of the man exists in his poetry. Certainly, many of us who have become acquainted with Emerson generally arrived at an understanding of his poetry through an understanding of his prose. If such an approach should seem to reflect the limitations of our own perceptions, or of Emerson's poetry, Frost has never been troubled by either one of these limitations—probably because his individual convictions predisposed him to an immediate recognition of Emerson's major premises as stated in his compressed and gnarled verse.

If, however, these two are to be considered critics of their times, why should they have any claim on us ? Why should we bother to give ear to their assertions which are not in accord with the doctrines of today's learned economists and sociologists. Perhaps because our economists and sociologists have not been able to solve today's problems ; but certainly because Emerson and Frost have undergone rigorous training in the processes of thought. At an early age they both discovered that abundant learning does not form the mind ; that the understanding of order and intelligence in the chaotic confusion and multiplicity of details in the modern world comes rather from the mastery of a few fundamentals. Their method of approach is akin to the method of solving a mathematical problem in complex fractions. The need, in each case, is for the perception of some common denominator which permits the recognition of values and relationships between the parts. To recognize such values and relationships is the first step in knowing how to handle them, how to cope with them.

Now the common denominator of the poet, which enables him to deal with the complex fractions of life, is the metaphor—a tool safe for calculation only in the hands of well trained experts. Before we may understand Emerson and Frost as critics of their times, we need to understand the particular way in which they use metaphor as a common denominator. Emerson makes his most coherent statement on this point in his well-known essay "Nature", from which I choose these sentences:

"Every naturul fact is a symbol of some spiritual fact... These are not the dreams of a few poets, here and there... man is an analogist, and studies relations in all objects... We are thus assisted by natural objects in the expression of particular meanings... The world is emblematic. Parts of speech are metaphors, because the whole of nature is a metaphor of the human mind. The laws of moral nature answer to those of matter as face to face and glass to glass ...Any distrust of the permanence of laws would paralyze the faculties of man... Man is hereby apprised that whilst the world is a spectacle, something in himself is stable."

So much for Emerson on the metaphor as a common denominator of understanding. Frost, on the other hand, has written a prose essay, which deserves to be better known, on "Education by Poetry." It is equally explicit, and I shall quote from it here:

"I do not think anybody ever knows the discreet use of metaphor, his own and other people's, and the discreet handling of metaphor, unless he has been properly educated in poetry... Unless you are at home in the metaphor, unless you have had your proper poetical education in the metaphor, you are not safe anywhere. Because you are not at ease in figurative values; you don't know the metaphor in its strength and its weakness. You don't know how far you may expect to ride it and when it may break down with you. You are not safe in science; you are not safe in history.

"Poetry provides the one permissible way of saying one thing and meaning another... Greatest of all attempts to say one thing in terms of another is the philosophical attempt to say matter in terms of spirit, or spirit in terms of matter, to make the final unity. That is the greatest attempt that ever failed. We stop just short there. But it is the height of poetry, the height of all thinking... that attempt to say matter in terms of spirit and spirit in terms of matter.

"It is wrong to call anybody a materialist simply because he tries to say spirit in terms of matter, as if that were a sin. Materialism is not the attempt to say *all* in terms of matter. The only materialist—be he poet, teacher, scientist, politician, or statesman—is the man who gets lost in his material without a gathering metaphor to throw it into shape and order. He is the lost soul."

Obviously, Emerson and Frost are in complete agreement as to the importance of the metaphor as a common denominator, as a method of reasoning

by which we may clarify fundamentals. And Emerson
carries the idea a step nearer to our goal when he
says, "I am a poet in the sense of a perceiver and
dear lover of the harmonies that are in the soul and
in matter—and specially of the correspondences between these and those." Thus we see what Emerson
meant when he said that he was a poet in theory,
ethics, and politics. He looked at each fact from
within and not merely as a reasoner who considered
outward manifestations. Like a careful mathemati-
cian he studied the relation of the parts to each
other, and searched for metaphors which might serve
accurately as common denominators to explain the
value, the relation, of part to part. All his reasoning sprang from these inner harmonies, as he called
them. And in this way he applied his basic doctrine
of fundamentals to solving the complexity of outward interests.

Always, as we shall see, both Emerson and Frost
express primary interest in whatever tends to pro-
mote the understanding of these inner harmonies
in the individual, in the private man. They look with
suspicion and distrust on any phenomenon, political
or economic, that tends to impede the growth of
these inner harmonies. Emerson and Frost seem to
say with other seers, "All other development is not
to the least purpose until you have developed wisdom and character thus, in human beings."

Such a final agreement between Frost and Emerson may seem the more striking if I am able to show, later, that each approaches this common ground of meeting from a diametrically opposite direction; that Emerson's concern for the supremacy of the individual grows out of a philosophic idealism which is essentially Platonic; that Frost's similar concern grows out of a skeptical realism which is impatient with the romantic dreaming of Platonism. Thus it seems more striking to discover that the two, approaching their final position in the Golden Mean from opposite directions, arrive at conclusions which are almost identical.

So much, then, by way of introduction.

THE America of Emerson's day was a picnic-land of opportunity for the individual. A new wave of pioneers had begun to find in the new West a fertile territory ripe for plunder. Emerson was conscious of the varied problems which developed with the Annexation of Texas, the Rush to California for gold, the question of slavery, the Civil War, and the building of the Union Pacific. Eight years before Emerson's death in 1882, Robert Frost was born in San Francisco and grew up to watch the fruition of so many of Emerson's hopes and fears for America —the complicity of problems which resulted from the aftermath of the frontier movement; the social

problems that developed through the growth of
monster cities, the conflicts between labor and capi-
tal, the era of great strikes, of great trusts, the Spanish
American War, the World War, reaction, panics, de-
pression, and loss of confidence for the individual.
It was inevitable that the America which produced
Emerson should have produced an optimist and an
idealist; it was almost as inevitable that the America
which produced Frost should have produced a skeptic and a realist. At the outset, however, Emerson
and Frost are agreed on one fundamental: the hope
for the individual and the nation in any time was
"man thinking," as Emerson put it. Emerson had
seen the need for this kind of wisdom in handling
the problems of expansion. At the age of 20 he had
considered the danger, when he wrote in his journal,

"The vast rapidity with which the deserts and for-
ests of the interior of this country are peopled have
led patriots to fear lest the nation grow *too fast* for its
virtue and its peace... Good men desire, and the
great cause of human nature demands, that this abundant overflowing richness wherewith God has blessed
this country be not misapplied and made a curse of
... How to effect the check proposed is an object
of momentous importance. And in view of an object of such magnitude, I know not who he is, that
can complain that motive is lacking in this latter
age, whereby men should become great."

Thus his persistent optimism was balanced by an instinctive caution which urged checks on any impatient change. His idealism was modified by a growing realism which led him to take up his middle ground position. "Human strength," he said, "is not in extremes, but in avoiding extremes." Again, "Place yourself in the middle of the stream of power and wisdom which animates all whom it floats, and you are without effort impelled to truth, to right, and a perfect contentment." A pretty idea, but unfortunately one more likely to be true in Emerson's time than in our own.

Even Emerson began early to recognize the current impatience with any middle course action which might be considered restraint. The bold and unscrupulous policies which grew out of President Andrew Jackson's administration aroused Emerson to a bitter denunciation. He attacked the growing disease which he called "shallow Americanism"; a disease especially prevalent in a young country and easily contagious. He described among its symptoms the desire to "get rich by credit. . . or skill without study, or mastery without apprenticeship, or the sale of goods through pretending that they sell, or power through making believe you are powerful. . . or wealth by fraud." He spoke out strongly against accepting such a state of things as inevitable and complained,

"We countenance each other in this life of show,

puffing, advertisement and manufacture of public opinion; and excellence is lost sight of in the hunger for sudden performance..."

Nevertheless, he recognized in Jacksonian democracy new possibilities for the individual man as opposed to the aristocrat, and once in his journal, as he mourned the "dearth of American genius," he dared hope that "the evil may be cured by this rank rabble party, the Jacksonism of the country, heedless of English, and of all literature—a stone cut out of the ground without hands;—they may root out the hollow dilletantism of our cultivation in the coarsest way, and the newborn may begin again to frame their own world with greater advantage."

But the fountain head of Emerson's persistent optimism was his belief in the individual, each potentially divine. "I cannot find language sufficient to convey my sense of the sacredness of private integrity," he wrote. "All men, all things, the state, the church, yea, the friends of the heart, are phantasms and unreal beside the sanctuary of the heart." And again, "In all my lectures I have taught one doctrine, namely, the infinitude of the private man... Leave this hypocritical prating about the masses. Masses are rude, unmade, pernicious in their demands and influence... I wish not to concede anything to them, but to... divide and break them up, and draw individuals out of them. I see plainly the fact that there is no progress to the race, that the progress is of the individuals."

What, then, did Emerson have to say about the intelligent individual in his relation to society? First that the individual should think of himself as a creator of government; that government, as the representative of the individual to society as a group, must be kept flexible enough to be adapted to the shifting demands placed upon it; that a primary demand placed upon government was that government should participate in the education of its citizens in numerous ways until the need for certain functions of the government would be decreased. His weakness here lay in his failure to realize that no amount of education could ever remove the necessity for an involved mechanism of government which should concern itself with the complicated inter-relationships of individuals, groups, states, regions, nations. Yet his vague idealism on this point was balanced by a practical admission that regardless of the equal rights of the individuals, no amount of laws could ever transform this ideal equality into a real equality. This he made clear in his criticism of such communal experiments as that which he watched at Brook Farm. In commenting on the Brook Farm proposal to keep equality by distributing wages equally, he wrote, ". . . not an instant would a dime remain a dime. In one hand it became an eagle as it fell, and in another hand a copper cent. For the whole value of the dime is in knowing what to do with it. One man buys with it a land-title of an Indian, and makes his posterity princes; or buys corn enough to feed the world; or pen, ink, and paper, or a painter's brush, by which he can communicate himself to the human race as if he were fire; and the other buys barley candy. Money is of no value; it cannot spend itself. All depends on the skill of the spender."

Nevertheless, this very inequality of talent required, in Emerson's eyes, the most thorough consideration of government, to avoid injustices of graft and greed; to curb the exploitation of the weak by the strong. And his suggestions here contained sharp criticism of existing government:

"The true offices of the State, the State has let fall to the ground; in the scramble of parties for the public purse, the main duties of government were omitted,—the duty to instruct the ignorant, to supply the poor with work and with good guidance. . . Yes, Government must educate the poor man. Look across the country from any hill-side around us and the landscape seems to crave Government. The actual differences of men must be acknowledged, and met with love and wisdom. These rising grounds which command the valley below, seem to ask for the lords, true lords, land-lords, who understand the land and its uses and the applicabilities of men, and whose government would be what it should, namely mediation between want and supply."

Suppose, however, that after such mediation had been made, to the best of government's ability, there still remained such obvious inequalities between wisdom and stupidity, industriousness and laziness, genius and dullness? Did Emerson mean that food should be put in the mouths of the stupid and lazy? Emerson was far too shrewd to let mercy grow into sentimentality. He was ready to be ruthless with any humanitarianism which went about its task in tears. The passage in "Self Reliance" which illustrates his hard-headedness on this point has seemed shocking to some champions of Emerson. But rather than shocking, the passage is the logical carrying out of Emerson's attitude towards those who, of their own free will, turn their backs on their own potentialities and expect that the world owes them a living. I quote:

"Your goodness must have some edge to it—else it is none. The doctrine of hatred must be preached, as the counteraction of the doctrine of love, when that pules and whines. . . Do not tell me, as a good man did to-day, of my obligation to put all poor men in good situations. Are they *my* poor? I tell thee, thou foolish philanthropist, that I grudge the dollar, the dime, the cent I give to such men as do not belong to me and to whom I do not belong. There is a class of persons to whom by all spiritual affinity I am bought and sold; for them I will go to prison if need be; but your miscellaneous popular charities; the education at college of fools; the building of meeting houses to the vain end to which many now stand; alms to sots, and the thousand-fold Relief Societies;— though I confess with shame I sometimes succumb and give the dollar, it is a wicked dollar, which by and by I shall have the manhood to withhold."

The careless thinker incorrectly interprets this passage as an ugly and selfish example of "rugged individualism." But let it be said again: Emerson's individualism is more discriminating than that; it urges selfishness as a palliative to the kind of sentimental humanitarianism that confuses mercy with justice. Obviously, Emerson's point here is merely a restatement of his consistent position in the Golden Mean.

V. F. Calverton, in his leftist treatise on *The Liberation of American Literature*, is quick to conclude that if Emerson had known anything of the works of Marx and the Marxian socialists, "the whole direction of his philosophy would have made him their instant opponent." In one sense, this is absolutely true; but not in that sense which his critic implies. Calverton does not seem to recognize Emerson's conviction that the individual, falling short as he generally does of his intended greatness, and caught in the complicated toils of social forces and movements stronger than the individual, must depend on government to regulate such social forces and movements with critical justice, hard as that may be. It was exactly because the government of Emerson's own time failed to deal boldly with the problem of "mediation between want and supply" that he criticized it.

Nevertheless, Emerson also recognized that the laws of nature revealed in themselves a ruthless and realistic communism which belittled and counteracted the impatient artificialities of man-made communism, eager to achieve its ideal by a kind of social rape which violated natural laws. He said as much in a rather elaborate passage which I quote from his essay, "The Young American":

"Gentlemen, there is a sublime and friendly Destiny by which the human race is guided—the race never dying, the individual never spared—to results affecting masses and ages. Men are narrow and selfish, but the Genius or Destiny is not narrow, but beneficent. It is not discovered in their calculated and voluntary activity, but in what befalls, with or without their design. Only what is inevitable interests us, and it turns out that love and good are inevitable, and in the course of things. That Genius has infused itself into nature. It indicates itself by a small excess of good, a small balance in brute facts always favorable to the side of reason. . .

"This Genius or Destiny is of the sternest administration, though rumors exist of its secret tenderness. It may be styled a cruel kindness, serving the whole even to the ruin of the member; a terrible communist, reserving all profits to the community, without dividend to individuals. Its law is, you shall have everything as a member, nothing to yourself. For Nature is the noblest engineer, yet uses a grinding economy, working up all that is wasted to-day into to-morrow's creation..."

And then Emerson goes on to criticize man's impatience with man-made poverty:

"That serene Power interposes the check upon the caprices and officiousness of our wills. Its charity is not our charity. One of its agents is our will, but that which expresses itself in our will is stronger than our will. We are very forward to help it, but it will not be accelerated. It resists our meddling, eleemosynary contrivances. We devise sumptuary and relief laws, but the principle of population is always reducing wages... We legislate against forestalling and monopoly; we would have a common granary for the poor; but the selfishness which hoards the corn for high price is the preventative of famine; and the law of self-preservation is surer policy than any legislation can be. We concoct eleemosynary systems, and it turns out that our charity increases pauperism. We inflate our paper currency, we repair

commerce with unlimited credit, and are presently
visited with unlimited bankruptcy."

Thus speaks a critic of the American scene who
should hardly have been called on, so far ahead, to
predict some of the experiments and failures, trials
and errors, which we have followed wistfully in the
various programs of the "New Deal." The plain conclusion is that Emerson recognized in the very evils
of selfish competition some of the very virtues which
justified its right to survive and flourish, with government protection on the one hand, and government regulation on the other hand. With Thoreau,
Emerson was saying, "To speak practically. . . I ask
for, not at once no government, but *at once* a better
government." He saw a nation lunging forward into
a deservedly great future, but a nation too eager for
rape of natural wealth to consider the wisest means
to an ultimate goal. In his optimism he was eager to
see the objectives set at their highest; he sang out to
America, "Hitch your wagon to a star," but at the
same time he was cautioning America to hitch that
wagon securely, lest the wagon be left behind. In the
pell-mell landslide towards materialism he was forever trying to plead for an equal enthusiasm for spiritual wealth and wisdom. This was exactly what he
had in mind when he wrote,

"Amidst the downward tendency and proneness of
things, when every voice is raised for a new road or

another statue or a subscription of stock;...for a
new house or a larger business; for a political party, or
the division of an estate; will you not tolerate one or
two solitary voices in the land, speaking for thoughts
and principles not marketable or perishable?"

ROBERT FROST's plea for a right to be heard is by
no means so insistent as Emerson's. If he, too,
champions the sacredness of the inner man, he lacks
Emerson's evangelical passion. At heart a skeptic,
he has always been impatient with the Platonic con-
cepts which influenced Emerson's thinking. Frost
once gave his own definition of Platonism in an a-
musing passage which had reference to his friendship
with Edwin Arlington Robinson—a poet, inciden-
tally, whose debt to Emerson was far greater than
Frost's, and whose kinship with Emerson's idealism
was far closer than Frost's kinship. Frost wrote,
"I am not the Platonist Robinson was. By Platonist
I mean one who believes what we have here is an imperfect copy of what is in heaven. The woman you
have is an imperfect copy of some woman in heaven
or in some one else's bed. Many of the world's greatest—maybe all of them—have been ranged on that
romantic side. I am philosophically opposed to having one Iseult for my vocation and another for my
avocation... Let me not sound the least bit smug. I
define a difference with proper humility. A truly gal-

lant Platonist will remain a bachelor as Robinson did from unwillingness to reduce any woman to the condition of being used without being idealized."

Although this witty protest reveals Frost's skepticism, his New England heritage of caution, moderation, and reticence permits the flexible reconciliation of conflicting beliefs in a Golden Mean. Generally he seems to me to hold a central position of skepticism without relinquishing faith, on the one hand or agnosticism, on the other hand. By limiting the functions of each he is able to make the three lie down together. Or, to change the figure, his skepticism acts as a balance-wheel which controls the accelerations of faith and the decelerations of agnosticism. Frost's middle course is thoroughly classical in its stoic moderation, but it is colored less by Stoicism than by the honest virtue and excellence of a genuinely mystical New England Puritanism—which perhaps is his direct heritage from the America of Emerson's day. Although he showed an early instinctive distaste for stereotyped religious formulas and ecclesiastical dogma, he also showed an instinctive acceptance of undefined beliefs in spiritual reality and unity. With Emerson he held that whoever would be a man must be a nonconformist; that nothing was sacred but the integrity of his own mind.

As products of the times in which they lived, both Frost and Emerson were fascinated by the new revelations of nineteenth century scientists concerning astronomy, geology, evolution. Each of them gathered in these new doctrines and accepted them not as shocking heresies but rather as sources for allegories, symbols, parables, metaphors. Each considered the findings of scientists to be in no sense a stumbling block to mystical belief in an evident design back of the universe. Frost's eclectic approach permitted him to select whatever he liked from the scientific philosophy of Darwin and Herbert Spencer. Certainly he rejected, to a large extent, the sense of futility of human effort which occurs in Spencer almost to the extent it occurs in Schopenhauer. He did not need to wait for Bergson and William James to help him reject Spencer's mechanistic and materialistic doctrines. In one of his most outspoken criticisms of modern bewilderment and sense of futility, Frost stated his position quite succinctly, and I select only a brief passage from his extended statement:

"All ages of the world are bad—a great deal worse anyway than Heaven. If they weren't the world might just as well be Heaven at once and have it over with. One can safely say after from six to thirty thousand years of experience that the evident design is a situation here in which it will always be about equally hard to save your soul. Whatever progress may be taken to mean, it can't mean making the world any easier a place in which to save your soul—or if you dislike hearing your soul mentioned in open meeting, say your decency, your integrity."

Immediately it becomes apparent that Frost, like Emerson, distrusts every other method of reform except that of awakening the soul to a sense of its possibilities, of its intended greatness. Conscious as he is of those involved problems which confront society, the masses, the nations, problems that must be tackled, he is primarily concerned with a new assertion of the old conviction that true progress and advance always has come from a few clear-thinking individuals. And so his concern is with the way in which the individual may gear and mesh mortal, finite life to a vast and deathless scheme.

Unlike Emerson, however, Frost lives in a time when the odds are stacked high against the individual, when opportunity is the exception and not the rule, when forces press so hard against the individual as to make him seem defeated before he starts. In recognizing these factors, Frost is neither an optimist nor a pessimist. His objective is to make the best of hardship even though the results may require a grim acceptance of gains that are little more than failures. Again and again he has used the stream-image in his poetry to illustrate his belief that we always live dangerously at the confluence of opposing forces that would destroy us, and that dangers are converted through struggle into strength. This idea is closely related to that of Bergson's evolutionary philosophy. And William James urged, similarly, a faith which should "offer the universe as an adventure rather than as a scheme."

Such beliefs, closely related to Frost's beliefs, explain his acceptance of a world which may seem too evil, too confused, too hopeless for some people. He speaks as one "acquainted with the night," and finds that the town clock "proclaimed the time was neither wrong nor right." He is ready to make the best of the worst because he finds that the worst lends itself to struggle; that somehow the individual must be fashioning from it some kind of defense against darkness and confusion. The salvation lies always in the individual, in his courage and daring when confronted with continual dangers—and that is why he has practical reasons for wanting dangers there; that is why he wants Heaven to leave Earth alone; since, as Frost and Hegel agree, the goal of life is not happiness but achievement.

The dangerous conflict is waged not merely for selfish ends or for an end in itself. Frost's poems contain repeated hints of his belief that man's physical and spiritual life are related to that larger spiritual realm beyond human comprehension. He believes that there is a higher form of experience in the universe than human experience; that we are, as James said, "merely tangent to curves of history, the beginnings and ends and forms of which pass wholly beyond our ken. . . tangents to the wider life of things."

Like Emerson, Frost accents the belief in free will, and in the belief that "the utmost reward of daring is still to dare." Also like Emerson, Frost states in his poetry that free will to choose may only heighten tragedy and sorrow rather than lessen it. Emerson pointed out that the widespread American doctrine of obeying the inner voice (the doctrine which guided men as diverse as John Brown and Brigham Young) was always being perverted. Rejecting the wild aberrations of the transcendentalists (with whom Emerson actually had nothing to do, although he is often mistakenly grouped with them), Emerson wrote, "Buddhism, Transcendentalism, life delights in reducing *ad absurdum.* The child, the infant, is a transcendentalist, and charms us all; we try to be, and instantly run in debt, lie, steal, commit adultery, go mad, and die."

For Emerson and Frost alike, the means of avoiding such perversions of free will were to be found in man's spiritual yearning toward even some partial understanding of the integrated relationship of disparate phenomena in all forms of life; the kinship of being that binds life into an intelligible whole; the discovery of common denominators which may strengthen faith in the one-ness of things.

At this stage, one is inclined to say to Frost, let us be specific. Let us have some example of human conduct which affords man defense against confusion, some example of action which enables us to live practically even when we are unable to grasp the direction and meaning of the so-called "intelligible whole." One of his poems contains a subtitle, "Resourcefulness is More than Understanding." The poem is a brief narrative of an episode in a zoo, a humorous picture of how a boy teased two monkeys in a cage by tickling and burning their noses with sunlight through a magnifying glass. The monkeys were perplexed. I quote:

> They stood arms laced together at the bars,
> And exchanged troubled glances over life.
> One put a thoughtful hand up to his nose
> As if reminded—or as if perhaps
> Within a million years of an idea.

After further teasing, the boy ventured too near, and "there was a sudden flash of arm" which gave the monkeys possession of the burning glass. Having given the curious object a brief study, the monkeys buried it carefully in their bedding straw and then

> Came dryly forward to the bars again
> To answer for themselves: Who said it mattered
> What monkeys did or didn't understand?

They might not understand a burning-glass.
They might not understand the sun itself.
It's knowing what to do with things that counts.

Here is a fresh statement of an old truth so pleas-
antly expressed in that provocative metaphor of
creatures who, like us, have come "perhaps within
a million years" of understanding. They thought of
something they could do without understanding—
and they did it. "Resourcefulness is more than understanding."

So many of Frost's poems touch on the theme of
doing; not merely for the sake of keeping one's hand
busy lest Satan should find mischief still, but rather
a doing which is related to an evident design, a doing
with thought and love of its own, to make a compre-
hensible little world within an incomprehensibly big
world. Two books which are old favorites with Frost
contain for him separate statements of this same
theme. They are *Robinson Crusoe* and *Walden*: rec-
ords of two different men in different situations; yet
each combined resourcefulness with a love of doing.
In mentioning these books as two of his favorites,
Frost stressed his pleasure in this relationship:

"*Robinson Crusoe* is never quite out of my mind.
I never tire of being shown how the limited can make
snug in the limitless. *Walden* has something of the
same fascination. Crusoe was cast away; Thoreau

was self-cast away. Both found themselves sufficient. No prose writer has ever been more fortunate in subject than these two."

In his poetry, Frost frequently hints at this general formula for defense against the confusion of a confused world. He reads the metaphor of Crusoe's experience thus: a man who accepts his situation in life and makes the best of what is at hand, without querulousness, impatience, and bitterness, can survive with a modicum of comfort and with considerable satisfaction—and can always be ready for something better when the opportunity is at hand.

Quite simply we have returned to the difference between the initial starting points of Frost and Emerson. Frost likes to think of people in two categories: those who visualize life at its best as perfection towards which people work; and those who visualize life as being nothing more or less than whatever they find it to be, good and bad enough to permit people to work crude material into some kind of form. The first group thinks of trying to overcome all drawbacks that hinder them from attaining perfection and eventually grow disappointed with their position, which they consider a compromise. The second group never uses the word compromise because there can not be any such position, so long as the best is done with whatever there is. This second viewpoint has its own idealism, of course; it presupposes that one cares to do the best he can. If then, compromise is made, it is a deliberate and self-imposed failure.

The first group is closely related to the Platonists; the second, to the skeptics of almost any age. In youth, Frost seems to say, most of us start out as Platonists. We believe in an ideal form of life for the individual, for society, for government, for the nations of the earth. We are willing to discard whatever is, in order to speed the establishment of the Kingdom of God on earth, as soon as we can. It seldom occurs to youth that God has any slow plan under way, and the young idealist can not see any inconsistency in growing impatient with God. Wanting short-cuts to Heaven, he believes his plan in execution is a divine inspiration which justifies a violence that is, in itself, contrary to natural law.

Eventually the idealist achieves, or fails, and settles down to enjoy, or resent, the consequences of his action. To be sure, he will not have much sympathy in later life for anyone who comes along with divine inspiration to execute by violence of word and deed another short-cut to Heaven. He must then raise new questions as to what is authority; as to what is right, and when. The result is usually confusion and bitterness.

Such is my understanding of Robert Frost's point of view. He summed up his own attitude so neatly in two lines that most people thought he was merely being playful and cute. But he was being humorous with a sad truth:

> I never dared be radical when young
> For fear of being a conservative when old.

He put it another way recently: "More than once I should have lost my soul to radicalism if it had been the originality it was mistaken for by its young converts."

All this clarifies his central position in the Golden Mean, with moderation in using one's resourcefulness to give shape and meaning to the raw materials of one's own life. The poet is using the metaphor of the artist's objective (the creation of form) as a symbol of the objective of any individual, since the process of giving shape to life is a selective one closely related to the selective process of art. The raw materials, the crudities of life, become assets rather than liabilities. The metaphors of evolution offer Frost models and patterns—the thrusting forward of living beings from the rolling clouds of nature so that in the forms of human beings, as he says, "nature reaches its height of form and through us exceeds itself." We, in turn, go on step by step, as we apply our own modest creative cunning to the unshaped possibilities about us to make forms which have their own meaning and beauty. We may start ever so simply and still find that in the very act of starting we are

"lost to the larger excruciations" which make life un-
bearable for those who prefer bewildered yearning
for the perfect forms and are disappointed with anything less than perfection. So long as the making of
form requires these raw materials for such making,
Frost willingly and realistically accepts the mixed
goodness and badness of life in all its crudity.

And how does Frost's individualism take into
consideration the relation of self to society? Much
as Emerson's did. Unless self is able to develop an
independent courage to walk alone, self will never
be of real value in mingling with others. Socrates
said it long ago: "Let him who would move the world
move first himself." And Frost criticizes his own age
in "Build Soil" when he writes, "We congregate em-
bracing from distrust as much as love, and too close
in to strike and be so very striking." "Build Soil" is
Frost's most extended utterance in poetry concerning the relation of the individual to society. He has
little to say about economic and social problems.
Instead, he stresses his conviction that the initial
reforms to be made, if any are to be lasting, are individual reforms. "To market 'tis our destiny to go,"
he admits, and he is glad that it is so; willing that
the "trial by market" and open competition should
always be the final test of success or failure. But in
preparation for the "trial by market", there must
be a long slow process of development, refinement,

growth, if the trial is to be met. And Frost points
out that in our eagerness to compete we come too
early with poor produce, physical, spiritual, mental.
Frost's metaphor is a modern version of Emerson's
doctrine of self reliance but it is an ageless one from
the farm: build and enrich the soil slowly for the
soil's sake first, without any impatient concern for
what may come of it. He adds, in the same poem:

> Keep off each other and keep each other off.
> You see the beauty of my proposal is
> It needn't wait on general revolution.
> I bid you to a one-man revolution—
> The only revolution that is coming.

It might be said that neighborliness is the keynote
of Frost's social outlook. The development of virtue, merit, and strength in the individual is not a
selfish goal to either Frost or Emerson, for they both
stress the unavoidable influence of life upon life.
But Frost protests that the idealism which has been
voiced down the ages from Athens to Brook Farm,
and back to Moscow, about the common brotherhood of man, is a romantic notion which may as
well be forgotten until individuals learn to live with
each other in the smallest community. The correc-
tive still rests with the individual:

> My friends all know I'm interpersonal.
> But long before I'm interpersonal

Away 'way down inside I'm personal.
Just so before we're international
We're national and act as nationals. . .
It's hard to tell which is the worse abhorrence
Whether it's persons pied or nations pied.
Don't let me seem to say the exchange, the
          encounter,
May not be the important thing at last.
It well may be.

Such a humorous bit of jesting at the expense of
the romantic idealism which calls impatiently for the
international brotherhood of man is a part of Frost's
sensibility. For his pains in adumbrating his impatience with the cheap idealism of the believers in the
get-social-quick programs, Frost was once called a
"counter revolutionary." If argument had degenerated
to name-calling, Frost said, he was willing to retaliate
by calling his leftist critic "a bargain-counter revolutionary."

Naturally, any excursion of the individual into
society—if only in the sense of neighborliness—quickly
brings questions of allegiance outside self; loyalties
to loved ones, to townspeople, to countrymen, to
downtrodden peoples. Our love makes us offer help
impulsively to those whose sorrow lays claim to
sympathy. Like Emerson, he says, it is difficult to
restrain the impulsive gesture of intended good al-

though it may not always prove to be the good intended. In one of his poems, "The Exposed Nest,"
Frost recalls covering the naked fledglings with grass
and thus scaring off the mother who might never
dare to return:

> We saw the risk we took in doing good,
> But dared not spare to do the best we could,
> Though harm should come of it...

There are several other poems which concern the
subject of Frost's excursions outside self into the
sufferings of others. One of the earliest poems, "Love
and a Question," is an unlocked metaphor. The
young bridegroom leaves his bride alone before the
fireplace to answer a knock on the cottage door; to
find a tramp asking for a night's lodging. There was
nowhere else for the stranger to go and the night
would be cold. Whose care was whose? How selfish
had love a right to be?

> The bridegroom thought it little to give
> A dole of bread, a purse,
> A heartfelt prayer for the poor of God,
> Or for the rich a curse;
> But whether or not a man was asked
> To mar the love of two
> By harboring woe in the bridal house,
> The bridegroom wished he knew.

The question is left unanswered. Certainly, Frost
has spent much time thinking of possible answers to
the question of whose care was whose, for he knew
many years of poverty. Pleasant as it may be now to
look back on such picturesque beginnings for a suc-
cessful poet, one should not forget the persistence of
those lean years through which Frost lived. They
should have colored his thinking with bitterness. But
he was never known to be resentful about finding
himself in a world he never made; never tried to
blame anyone by guessing who or what was at fault.
He never hoped far ahead, and was too sensible to
think that the world owed him a living. Those early
years, hard and spotted with tragedy, are important
here only because some may think that Frost's deliberate weighing between reasonable justice and sentimental mercy is mere selfishness. But Frost, whose
first interest in politics led him to take sides as a
strong Cleveland Democrat, was still poor when he
first began to hate professional poverty. While yet a
farmer, with no good prospects, he was asked to
speak to a kind of Junior League group trying to
raise money for the poor. He took as his text, "Let
not man bring together what God hath set asunder"
—let the rich keep away from the poor. He added,
"It says in the Bible, you think—I don't—it says in
the Bible that you always have the poor with you.
That isn't what it says. It says, 'For Christ's sake,

forget the poor some of the time.' There are many beautiful things in the world besides poverty."

Here is bitterness, not against the rich or poor, but against the professional show of either for boastfulness or for gain. And Frost has been outspoken in his criticism of those government programs which encourage professional poverty on the one hand and professional "greedy good-doers" on the other hand. In "A Roadside Stand," he describes the ineffectual wistfulness of the country people who hope their roadside stand will bring in a little extra money; and this recalls projected legislation which will end such wistfulness:

> It is in the news that all these pitiful kin
> Are to be bought out and mercifully gathered in
> To live in villages next to the theatre and store
> Where they won't have to think for themselves
>   any more;
> While greedy good-doers, beneficent beasts of
>   prey,
> Swarm over their lives enforcing benefits
> That are calculated to soothe them out of their
>   wits,
> And by teaching them how to sleep the sleep all
>   day,
> Destroy their sleeping at night the
>   ancient way.

The poem ends with Frost's wondering how it would
be to have the relief-tables turned:

> I can't help owning the great relief it would be
> To put these people at one stroke out of their
>   pain.
> And then next day as I came back into the sane,
> I wonder how I should like you to come to me
> And offer to put me gently out of my pain.

It is a restatement of the old rule, "Do unto others".
It is another way of raising the old question as to
which comes first, mercy or justice. With Frost we
return, in any such consideration, to his metaphor
of life that exists dangerously at the confluence of
streams of opposites, so that each of us is constantly
required to "sway playfully and vitally" somewhere
between the opposites which try vainly to destroy
each other—and which are capable of destroying us.
The conflict between opposing goods is of more
interest to him than the conflicts between good and
bad, for he looks on the first as real tragedy and on
the second conflict as tending always towards melo-
drama, with a villain too conveniently there to be
blamed. He makes this point nicely in his remarks
"To a Young Wretch" who has cut a Christmas tree
from his woods without asking permission:

> It is your Christmasses against my woods,
> But even where thus opposing interests kill,

They are to be thought of as conflicting goods
Oftener than as conflicting good and ill;
Which makes the war god seem no special dunce
For always fighting on both sides at once.

Obviously, no opposing goods are more dangerous
to each other and to the individual or society than
the heart and the mind. Yet each needs the other to
counterbalance extremes. The rational position of
the Golden Mean requires that justice should be
given a little precedence over the emotionally well-
meaning and confusing goodness of mercy. Frost is
annoyed at times because people would eagerly protect our right to succeed—and refuse to protect our
right to fail. If it becomes illegal to fail, he points
out, it will be because our humanitarianism has
slopped over into sentimentality.

Frost does not mean to imply that mercy has no
place in the laws of organized society. He believes
in the importance of those laws which keep us from
being too free for our own good, and recalls, in
"Build Soil", that we have put important curbs on
the freedom to be too selfish:

Everyone asks for freedom for himself,
The man free love, the business man free trade,
The writer and talker free speech and free press.
Political ambition has been taught,
By being punished back, it is not free;

It must at some point gracefully refrain.
Greed has been taught a little abnegation
And it shall be more before we're done with it.
It is just fool enough to think itself
Self-taught. But our brute snarling and lashing
   taught it.

FOR my own part, I wish only to state that it would be comforting for some of the rest of us if we could share the vision of such seers as Frost and Emerson; if we could believe that the dice of God are always loaded and that the power of the forces of good is just a bit stronger than the power of the forces of evil. Some of us are even willing to agree that good eventually triumphs. Unfortunately, however, the particular genius of evil is to marshal its forces with such cunning that it can achieve power enough to stand off and out-maneuver the forces of good for months and years and decades. For that reason, there can never be any complacency about the eventual outcome, unless individuals and governments exert themselves unceasingly to combat the problems forever attractive to the forces of evil. And on this general point I am sure that Emerson and Frost are agreed. On the matter of specifics to solve the problems of society and government, both Frost and Emerson are particularly weak. But, as I said at the start, so also are the sociologists and the economists.

In conclusion, we may easily guess what our two poets would have to say about the relative merits of our two major political parties as they exist in 1940. Now that Frost is living on top of Beacon Hill in Boston, it is pleasant to imagine that on this very evening he may meet the ghost of Emerson in the familiar shadows of Boston Common. If they should stop to talk, they could not leave politics alone. There would be no bitterness in their cautious weighing of merits. Quite properly, they would spend considerable time defining the apparent differences between the New Dealers and the Old Guard. But finally they would get down to their favorite topic: which political viewpoint would seem to offer the best opportunity to America for continuing its destiny? Which would seem to create the best and the most honest opportunity for the individual? Realistic in their approach, they would weigh the evils of Republican craving for private enterprise, private profit, private greed, professional private wealth and private failure, against the evils of New Deal craving for public enterprise, public profit, public greed, professional public poverty and public failure. Then they would shake their heads, smile at each other sadly, and agree that the lesser of the two evils would be represented by the Old Guard.

Two hundred and fifty copies, printed by
Edmund Thompson at Hawthorn House,
Windham, Connecticut, were completed
on the last day of the year nineteen
hundred and forty.

The type is Bulmer,
hand set; the paper, Worthy Charta.
The portrait of Emerson is from a wood-
cut by James Britton, and is used through
the courtesy of Edwin Valentine Mitchell.

57